THIS JOURNAL BELONGS TO:

_____

DATE:

TIME:

LOCATION:

WEATHER:

METHOD:

🐟 CATCH INFORMATION

_____

_____

_____

_____

_____

_____

NOTES & SKETCHES

DATE:

TIME:

LOCATION:

WEATHER:

METHOD:

🐟 CATCH INFORMATION

NOTES & SKETCHES

DATE:

TIME:

LOCATION:

WEATHER:

METHOD:

🐟 CATCH INFORMATION

_____
_____
_____
_____
_____
_____
_____

NOTES & SKETCHES

DATE:

TIME:

LOCATION:

WEATHER:

METHOD:

🐟 CATCH INFORMATION

✏ NOTES & SKETCHES

DATE:

TIME:

LOCATION:

WEATHER:

METHOD:

🐟 CATCH INFORMATION

_____

_____

_____

_____

_____

_____

_____

NOTES & SKETCHES

DATE:

TIME:

LOCATION:

WEATHER:

METHOD:

🐟 CATCH INFORMATION

_____
_____
_____
_____
_____
_____
_____

NOTES & SKETCHES

DATE:

TIME:

LOCATION:

WEATHER:

METHOD:

🐟 CATCH INFORMATION

_____

_____

_____

_____

_____

_____

_____

🖉 NOTES & SKETCHES

DATE:

TIME:

LOCATION:

WEATHER:

METHOD:

CATCH INFORMATION

_____

_____

_____

_____

_____

_____

_____

NOTES & SKETCHES

DATE:

TIME:

LOCATION:

WEATHER:

METHOD:

🐟 CATCH INFORMATION

NOTES & SKETCHES

DATE:

TIME:

LOCATION:

WEATHER:

METHOD:

🐟 CATCH INFORMATION

_____
_____
_____
_____
_____
_____
_____

NOTES & SKETCHES

DATE:

TIME:

LOCATION:

WEATHER:

METHOD:

🐟 CATCH INFORMATION

_____
_____
_____
_____
_____
_____
_____

NOTES & SKETCHES

DATE:

TIME:

LOCATION:

WEATHER:

METHOD:

🐟 CATCH INFORMATION

_____
_____
_____
_____
_____
_____
_____

NOTES & SKETCHES

DATE:

TIME:

LOCATION:

WEATHER:

METHOD:

CATCH INFORMATION

📝 NOTES & SKETCHES

DATE:

TIME:

LOCATION:

WEATHER:

METHOD:

CATCH INFORMATION

NOTES & SKETCHES

DATE:

TIME:

LOCATION:

WEATHER:

METHOD:

🐟 CATCH INFORMATION

NOTES & SKETCHES

DATE:

TIME:

LOCATION:

WEATHER:

METHOD:

🐟 CATCH INFORMATION

_____
_____
_____
_____
_____
_____
_____
_____

NOTES & SKETCHES

DATE:

TIME:

LOCATION:

WEATHER:

METHOD:

🐟 CATCH INFORMATION

_____

_____

_____

_____

_____

_____

_____

✏ NOTES & SKETCHES

DATE:

TIME:

LOCATION:

WEATHER:

METHOD:

🐟 CATCH INFORMATION

NOTES & SKETCHES

DATE:

TIME:

LOCATION:

WEATHER:

METHOD:

🐟 CATCH INFORMATION

NOTES & SKETCHES

DATE:

TIME:

LOCATION:

WEATHER:

METHOD:

CATCH INFORMATION

NOTES & SKETCHES

DATE:

TIME:

LOCATION:

WEATHER:

METHOD:

🐟 CATCH INFORMATION

NOTES & SKETCHES

DATE:

TIME:

LOCATION:

WEATHER:

METHOD:

🐟 CATCH INFORMATION

_____

_____

_____

_____

_____

_____

_____

NOTES & SKETCHES

DATE:

TIME:

LOCATION:

WEATHER:

METHOD:

🐟 CATCH INFORMATION

NOTES & SKETCHES

DATE:

TIME:

LOCATION:

WEATHER:

METHOD:

🐟 CATCH INFORMATION

NOTES & SKETCHES

DATE:

TIME:

LOCATION:

WEATHER:

METHOD:

🐟 CATCH INFORMATION

NOTES & SKETCHES

DATE:

TIME:

LOCATION:

WEATHER:

METHOD:

🐟 CATCH INFORMATION

_____
_____
_____
_____
_____
_____
_____

✏ NOTES & SKETCHES

DATE:

TIME:

LOCATION:

WEATHER:

METHOD:

🐟 CATCH INFORMATION

_____
_____
_____
_____
_____
_____
_____

✎ NOTES & SKETCHES

DATE:

TIME:

LOCATION:

WEATHER:

METHOD:

🐟 CATCH INFORMATION

NOTES & SKETCHES

DATE:

TIME:

LOCATION:

WEATHER:

METHOD:

🐟 CATCH INFORMATION

_____
_____
_____
_____
_____
_____
_____

✏ NOTES & SKETCHES

DATE:

TIME:

LOCATION:

WEATHER:

METHOD:

🐟 CATCH INFORMATION

_____

_____

_____

_____

_____

_____

_____

NOTES & SKETCHES

DATE:

TIME:

LOCATION:

WEATHER:

METHOD:

🐟 CATCH INFORMATION

NOTES & SKETCHES

DATE:

TIME:

LOCATION:

WEATHER:

METHOD:

🐟 CATCH INFORMATION

_____

_____

_____

_____

_____

_____

_____

NOTES & SKETCHES

DATE:

TIME:

LOCATION:

WEATHER:

METHOD:

🐟 CATCH INFORMATION

_____
_____
_____
_____
_____
_____
_____
_____

NOTES & SKETCHES

DATE:

TIME:

LOCATION:

WEATHER:

METHOD:

🐟 CATCH INFORMATION

NOTES & SKETCHES

DATE:

TIME:

LOCATION:

WEATHER:

METHOD:

🐟 CATCH INFORMATION

NOTES & SKETCHES

DATE:

TIME:

LOCATION:

WEATHER:

METHOD:

🐟 CATCH INFORMATION

NOTES & SKETCHES

DATE:

TIME:

LOCATION:

WEATHER:

METHOD:

🐟 CATCH INFORMATION

_____
_____
_____
_____
_____
_____
_____

NOTES & SKETCHES

DATE:

TIME:

LOCATION:

WEATHER:

METHOD:

🐟 CATCH INFORMATION

_____

_____

_____

_____

_____

_____

_____

NOTES & SKETCHES

DATE:

TIME:

LOCATION:

WEATHER:

METHOD:

🐟 CATCH INFORMATION

NOTES & SKETCHES

DATE:

TIME:

LOCATION:

WEATHER:

METHOD:

🐟 CATCH INFORMATION

_____

_____

_____

_____

_____

_____

_____

NOTES & SKETCHES

DATE:

TIME:

LOCATION:

WEATHER:

METHOD:

🐟 CATCH INFORMATION

_____

_____

_____

_____

_____

_____

_____

NOTES & SKETCHES

DATE:

TIME:

LOCATION:

WEATHER:

METHOD:

🐟 CATCH INFORMATION

NOTES & SKETCHES

DATE:

TIME:

LOCATION:

WEATHER:

METHOD:

🐟 CATCH INFORMATION

_____

_____

_____

_____

_____

_____

_____

NOTES & SKETCHES

DATE:

TIME:

LOCATION:

WEATHER:

METHOD:

CATCH INFORMATION

_____
_____
_____
_____
_____
_____
_____

NOTES & SKETCHES

DATE:

TIME:

LOCATION:

WEATHER:

METHOD:

🐟 CATCH INFORMATION

NOTES & SKETCHES

DATE:

TIME:

LOCATION:

WEATHER:

METHOD:

🐟 CATCH INFORMATION

_____

_____

_____

_____

_____

_____

_____

NOTES & SKETCHES

DATE:

TIME:

LOCATION:

WEATHER:

METHOD:

🐟 CATCH INFORMATION

_____
_____
_____
_____
_____
_____
_____

NOTES & SKETCHES

DATE:

TIME:

LOCATION:

WEATHER:

METHOD:

🐟 CATCH INFORMATION

_____
_____
_____
_____
_____
_____
_____

NOTES & SKETCHES

DATE:

TIME:

LOCATION:

WEATHER:

METHOD:

🐟 CATCH INFORMATION

_____
_____
_____
_____
_____
_____
_____

NOTES & SKETCHES

DATE:

TIME:

LOCATION:

WEATHER:

METHOD:

CATCH INFORMATION

NOTES & SKETCHES

DATE:

TIME:

LOCATION:

WEATHER:

METHOD:

🐟 CATCH INFORMATION

NOTES & SKETCHES

DATE:

TIME:

LOCATION:

WEATHER:

METHOD:

🐟 CATCH INFORMATION

NOTES & SKETCHES

DATE:

TIME:

LOCATION:

WEATHER:

METHOD:

🐟 CATCH INFORMATION

_____
_____
_____
_____
_____
_____
_____

NOTES & SKETCHES

DATE:

TIME:

LOCATION:

WEATHER:

METHOD:

🐟 CATCH INFORMATION

NOTES & SKETCHES

DATE:

TIME:

LOCATION:

WEATHER:

METHOD:

🐟 CATCH INFORMATION

_____
_____
_____
_____
_____
_____
_____

NOTES & SKETCHES

DATE:

TIME:

LOCATION:

WEATHER:

METHOD:

🐟 CATCH INFORMATION

NOTES & SKETCHES

DATE:

TIME:

LOCATION:

WEATHER:

METHOD:

🐟 CATCH INFORMATION

NOTES & SKETCHES

DATE:

TIME:

LOCATION:

WEATHER:

METHOD:

🐟 CATCH INFORMATION

_____
_____
_____
_____
_____
_____
_____
_____

NOTES & SKETCHES

DATE:

TIME:

LOCATION:

WEATHER:

METHOD:

🐟 CATCH INFORMATION

_____

_____

_____

_____

_____

_____

_____

& NOTES & SKETCHES

DATE:

TIME:

LOCATION:

WEATHER:

METHOD:

🐟 CATCH INFORMATION

NOTES & SKETCHES

DATE:

TIME:

LOCATION:

WEATHER:

METHOD:

🐟 CATCH INFORMATION

_____
_____
_____
_____
_____
_____
_____

NOTES & SKETCHES

DATE:

TIME:

LOCATION:

WEATHER:

METHOD:

🐟 CATCH INFORMATION

_____

_____

_____

_____

_____

_____

_____

_____

NOTES & SKETCHES

DATE:

TIME:

LOCATION:

WEATHER:

METHOD:

🐟 CATCH INFORMATION

NOTES & SKETCHES

DATE:

TIME:

LOCATION:

WEATHER:

METHOD:

🐟 CATCH INFORMATION

_____
_____
_____
_____
_____
_____
_____

NOTES & SKETCHES

DATE:

TIME:

LOCATION:

WEATHER:

METHOD:

🐟 CATCH INFORMATION

NOTES & SKETCHES

DATE:

TIME:

LOCATION:

WEATHER:

METHOD:

🐟 CATCH INFORMATION

NOTES & SKETCHES

DATE:

TIME:

LOCATION:

WEATHER:

METHOD:

🐟 CATCH INFORMATION

_____
_____
_____
_____
_____
_____
_____

NOTES & SKETCHES

DATE:

TIME:

LOCATION:

WEATHER:

METHOD:

🐟 CATCH INFORMATION

_____

_____

_____

_____

_____

_____

_____

_____

NOTES & SKETCHES

DATE:

TIME:

LOCATION:

WEATHER:

METHOD:

🐟 CATCH INFORMATION

NOTES & SKETCHES

DATE:

TIME:

LOCATION:

WEATHER:

METHOD:

🐟 CATCH INFORMATION

_____
_____
_____
_____
_____
_____
_____

NOTES & SKETCHES

DATE:

TIME:

LOCATION:

WEATHER:

METHOD:

🐟 CATCH INFORMATION

_____
_____
_____
_____
_____
_____
_____
_____

NOTES & SKETCHES

DATE:

TIME:

LOCATION:

WEATHER:

METHOD:

🐟 CATCH INFORMATION

NOTES & SKETCHES

DATE:

TIME:

LOCATION:

WEATHER:

METHOD:

🐟 CATCH INFORMATION

_____
_____
_____
_____
_____
_____
_____

NOTES & SKETCHES

DATE:

TIME:

LOCATION:

WEATHER:

METHOD:

🐟 CATCH INFORMATION

_____
_____
_____
_____
_____
_____
_____

NOTES & SKETCHES

DATE:

TIME:

LOCATION:

WEATHER:

METHOD:

🐟 CATCH INFORMATION

CPSIA information can be obtained
at www.ICGtesting.com
Printed in the USA
LVOW04s1454051216
515885LV00048B/2830/P

9 781535 091558